ingrid michaelson
girls and boys
including songs from *Be OK*

DEBORAH LOPEZ

This book was approved by Ingrid Michaelson

Piano/vocal arrangements by John Nicholas

Cherry Lane Music Company
Director of Publications/Project Editor: Mark Phillips
Project Coordinator: Rebecca Skidmore

ISBN 978-1-60378-225-8

Copyright © 2010 Cherry Lane Music Company
International Copyright Secured   All Rights Reserved

The music, text, design and graphics in this publication are protected by copyright law. Any duplication or transmission, by any means, electronic, mechanical, photocopying, recording or otherwise, is an infringement of copyright.

Visit our website at www.cherrylaneprint.com

DEBORAH LOPEZ

ingrid michaelson
girls and boys

Not long ago, Ingrid Michaelson's career assets amounted to little more than what *The New York Times* described as "a MySpace page and a dream." But her finely wrought, emotionally powerful songs have since set the music world on its ear.

A Staten Island native born to a sculptor mother and a classical-composer father, she began piano lessons at age four. But it was the family LP collection — stocked with midcentury pop, folk, and musicals — that first shaped her artistic sensibility. "I didn't grow up listening to the radio; I listened to my parents' records," she explains. "Everyone else had a crush on one of the New Kids on the Block, and I had a crush on Bing Crosby."

She didn't truly take up songwriting until after college. While touring the country in a theater troupe, she devoted every spare minute to penning the songs that would eventually comprise her album, *Girls and Boys*.

"That was a cool feeling, because I really worked at my writing," she says. "As a younger person, I was super melody-driven; then, somewhere along the way, I realized lyrics were just as important. I always knew when a song was catchy, but it took awhile to realize when a song would truly resonate with people."

She also credits groundbreaking work by other artists in the germination of *Girls and Boys*. "I feel like a lot of these songs happened when I stopped worrying what I thought people expected from me and when I started to be fearless," she reflects. "After listening to Regina Spektor's *Soviet Kitsch* in the summer of 2004 I was inspired beyond belief. Then I was given a copy of *Transatlanticism* by Death Cab for Cutie and my mind was blown into bits. Those two records helped me to realize that I could write about whatever I wanted — that I didn't have to be some barefoot, weeping female troubadour. It was liberating."

Her liberation from expectations had unexpected consequences. The makers of *Grey's Anatomy*, for example, placed Ingrid's track "Breakable" in an episode of the top-rated TV series after finding her on MySpace.

This exposure put her on the national map, and her songs started popping up more often on the series. "Corner of Your Heart" was followed by "Keep Breathing," which was used for the cathartic climax of the 2007 season finale (which reached more than 25 million viewers). Ingrid's track "The Way I Am," meanwhile, was featured in Old Navy's Fair Isle sweaters campaign.

As a result, she's taken these and other songs to new crowds nationwide, both as headliner and as support for artists like Dave Matthews Band and Jason Mraz. But no matter the venue, Ingrid's stage presence has retained the quirky, self-effacing charm and humor that won over audiences at her earliest club shows.

Even so, she marvels at the changes she's experienced. "I made *Girls and Boys* over the course of a year," she recalls. "We were in the studio maybe eight times total; there was no pressure. I never expected to sell a million singles of my tiny song. I'm still amazed that a song that has the word 'Rogaine' in it did so well!"

DEBORAH LOPEZ

Ingrid adds that her debut album "was a record born of innocence and sweet ignorance.

I knew nothing of the man behind the curtain — radio, record labels, touring. Now I know too much!" Fortunately, the innocent spirit informing that album was captured for posterity.

A Note About Be OK…

Ingrid says *Be OK*, which combines covers, live tracks, and a passel of new songs, was intended to tide audiences over until she completed a second full-length album (that set, *Everybody*, was released in 2009).

"I wanted to put something out as a gift to my fans," she says. "I still feel funny saying the word *fans*, but people who've responded really strongly to my music know a lot of these songs because they've heard me play them live. A lot of people have said they really wanted to be able to have them to listen to, and I wanted to give them that."

She opted to donate a portion of the proceeds from the sale of *Be OK* to Stand Up to Cancer, a group that's already used the title track on its website, where tens of thousands of visitors have been uplifted by its message.

"I met two of the women at Stand Up to Cancer and they were looking for songs," Ingrid says of her involvement with the organization. "I hadn't recorded it yet, so I sat in this little room and played "Be OK" for them, and by the end, we were all crying. It may sound hokey, but everybody who was there can testify to how magical the moment was."

She captures that magic just as beautifully on the studio version of "Be OK," as well as the other originals she unspools on the CD. Take the disc-closing "You and I," a charmingly retro ditty on which she sings of reaching for the brass ring — and of her desire to "get rich and give everybody nice sweaters and teach them how to dance."

DEBORAH LOPEZ

contents

6 die alone
15 masochist
23 breakable
29 the hat
38 the way i am
43 overboard
51 glass
55 starting now
64 corner of your heart
70 december baby
80 highway
87 far away

bonus songs from be ok

95 be ok
99 giving up
106 lady in spain
111 keep breathing
117 oh what a day
121 you and i

Die Alone

Words and Music by
Ingrid Michaelson

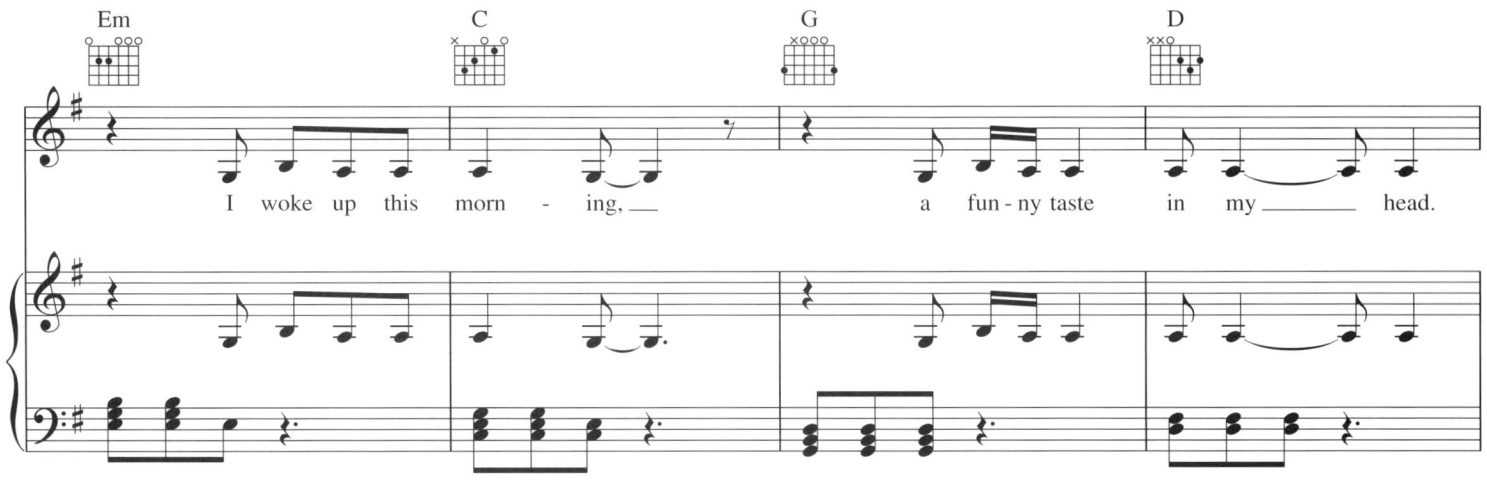

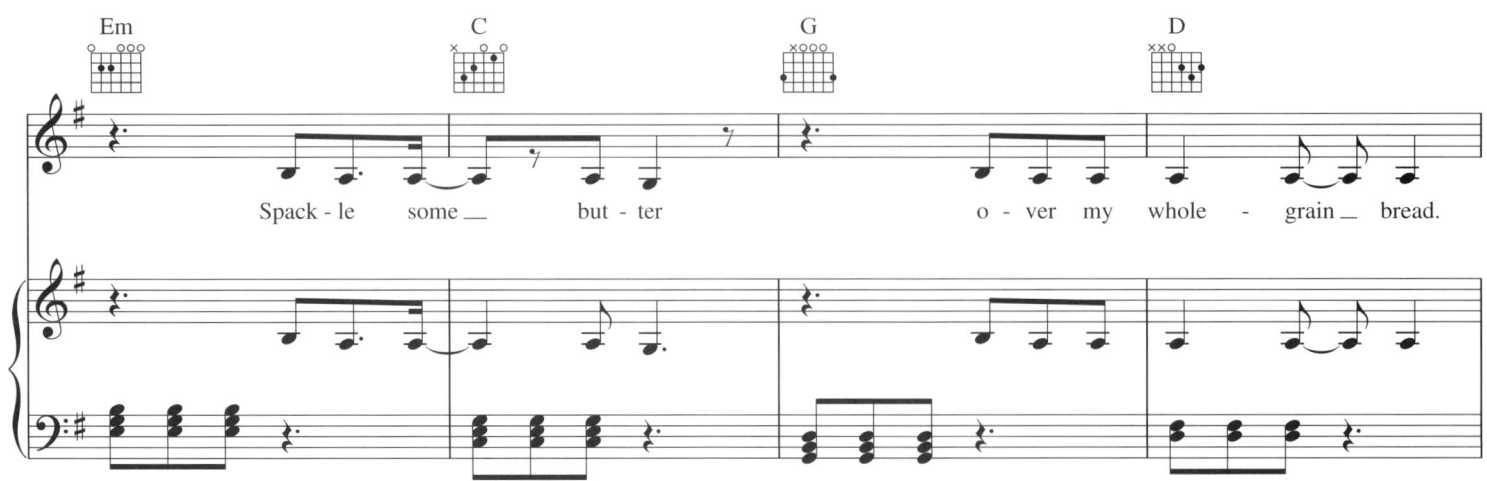

Copyright © 2006 Cabin 24 Records (ASCAP)
International Copyright Secured   All Rights Reserved

Masochist

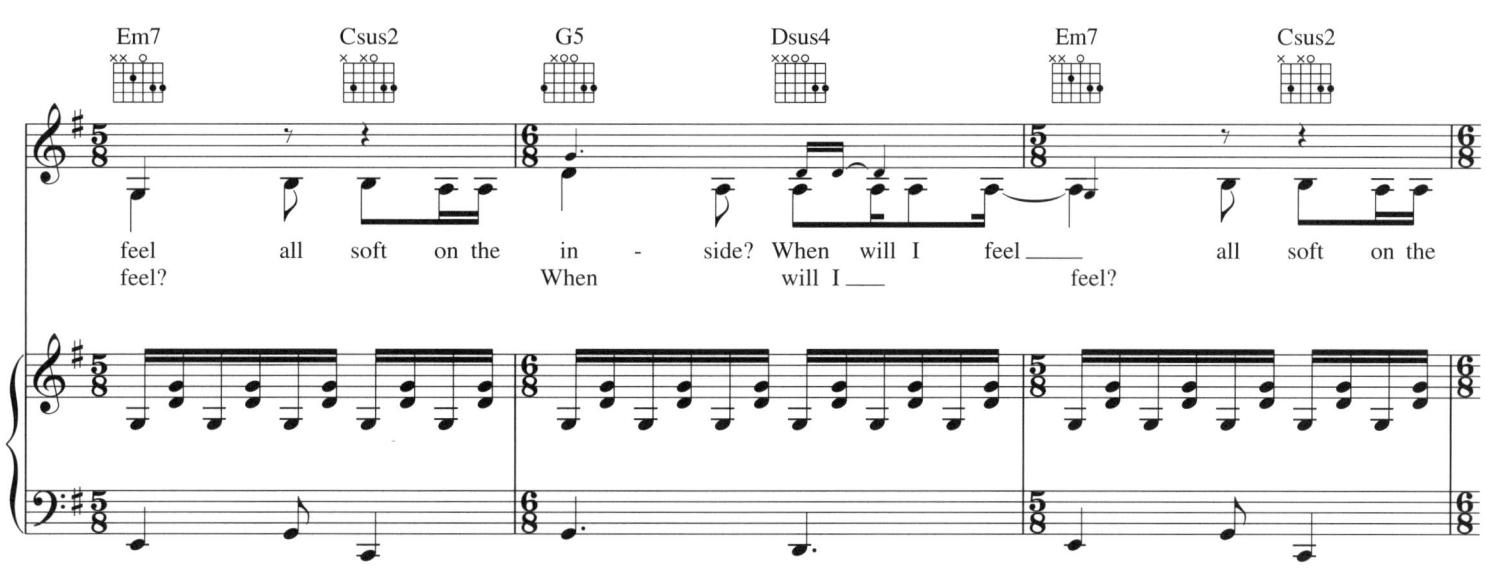
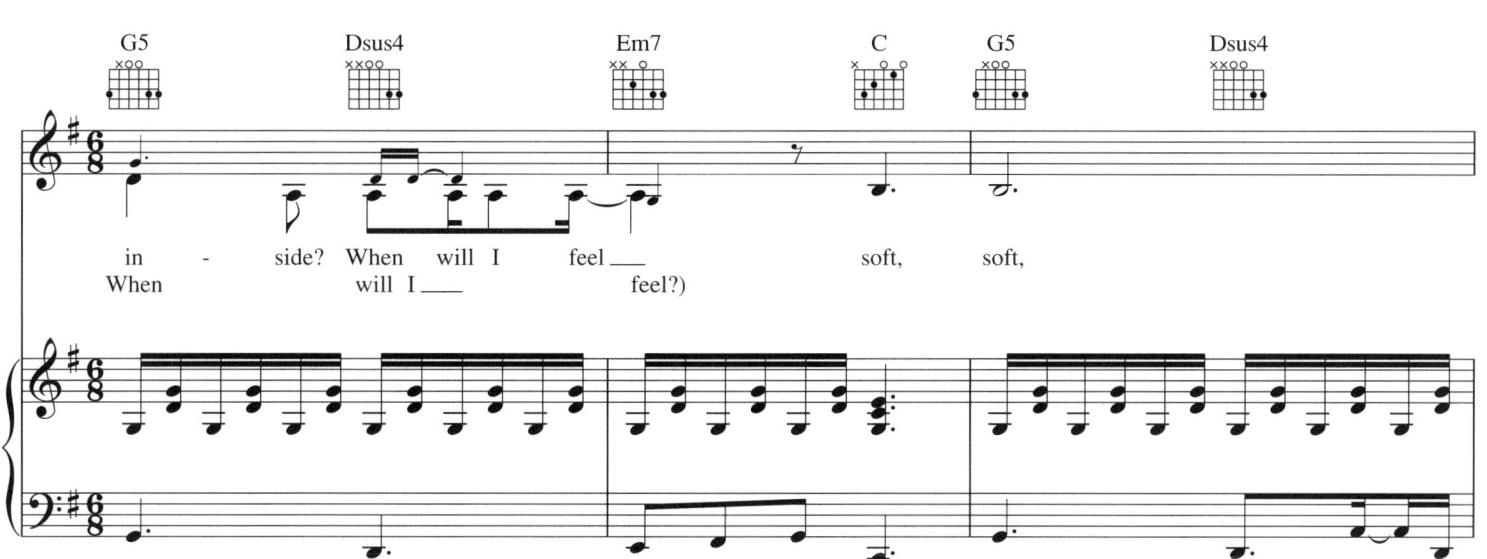

Breakable

Words and Music by
Ingrid Michaelson

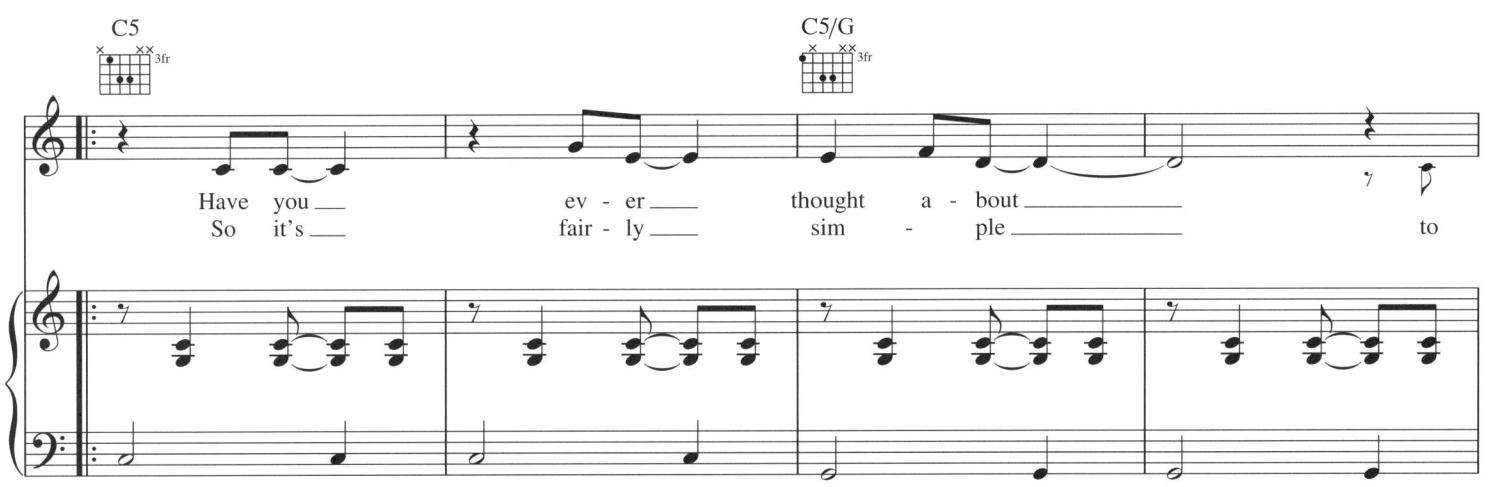
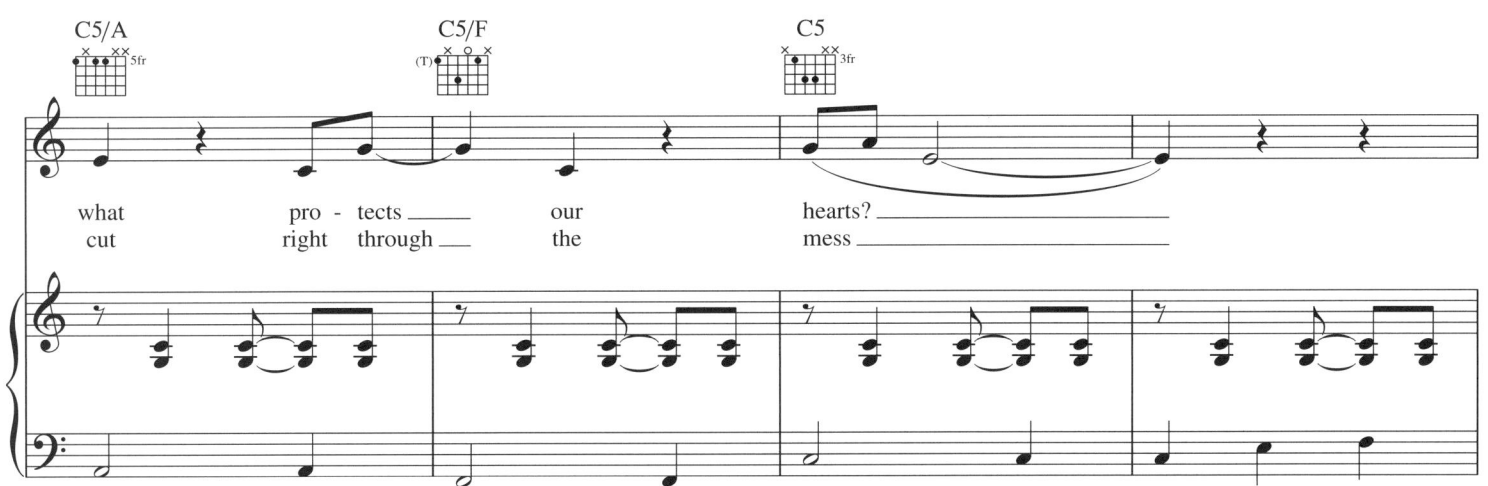

Copyright © 2006 Cabin 24 Records (ASCAP)
International Copyright Secured   All Rights Reserved

The Hat

Words and Music by
Ingrid Michaelson

30

The Way I Am

Overboard

Words and Music by
Ingrid Michaelson

43

Glass

Words and Music by
Ingrid Michaelson

Starting Now

Words and Music by
Ingrid Michaelson

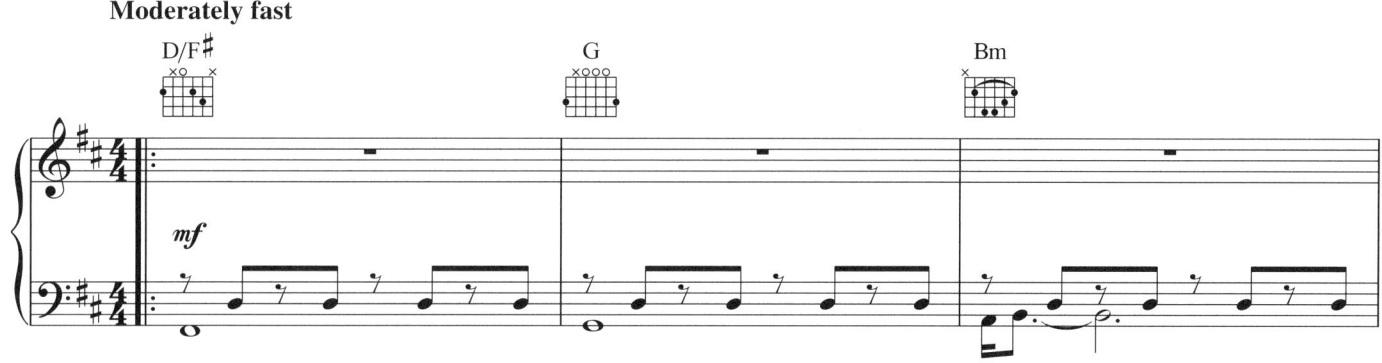

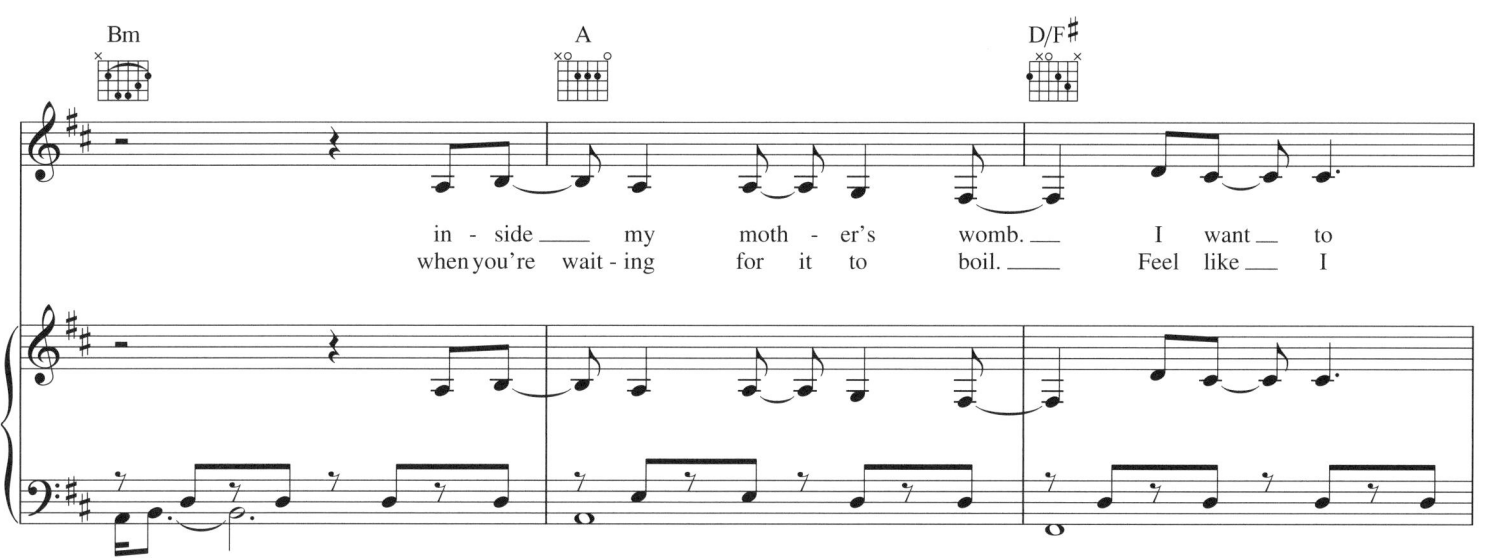

I want to crawl back inside my mother's womb. I want to
So life moves slowly when you're waiting for it to boil. Feel like I

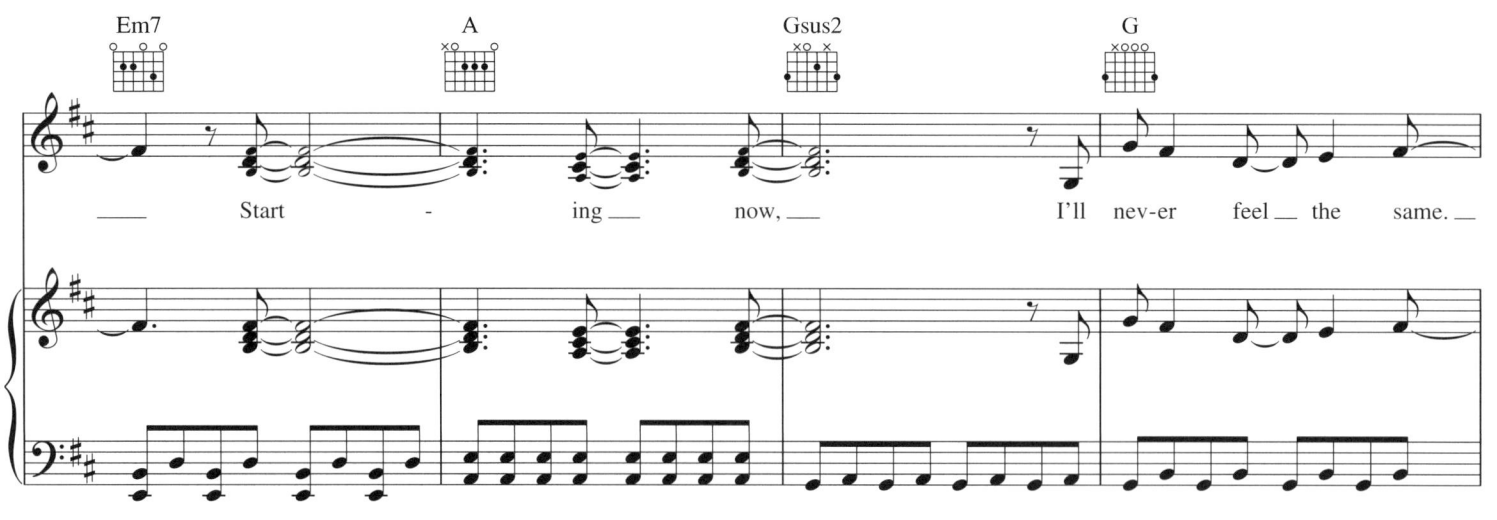
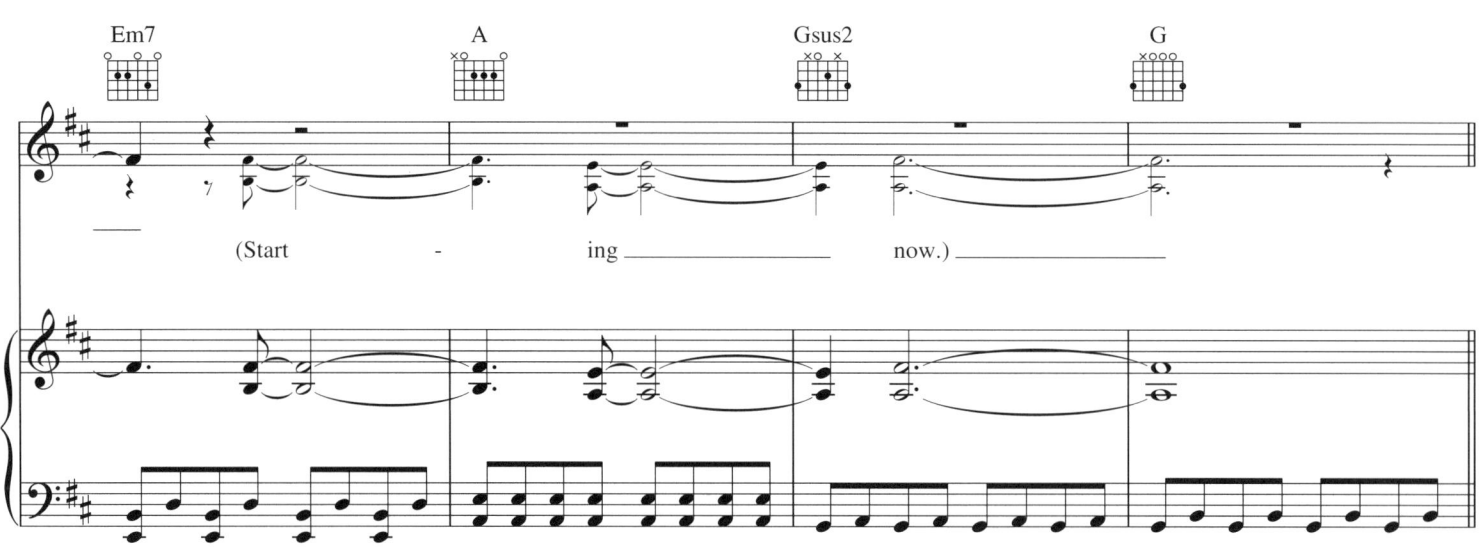
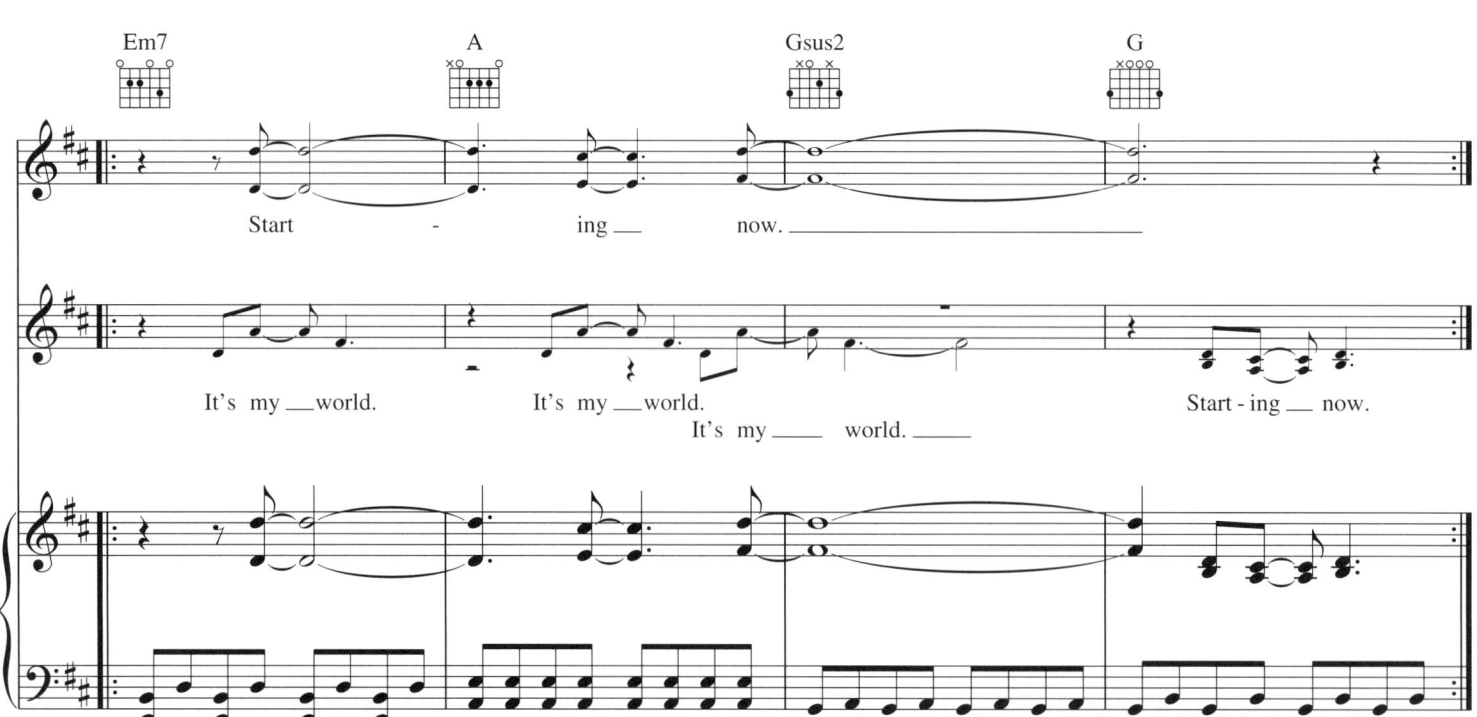

Corner of Your Heart

Words and Music by
Ingrid Michaelson

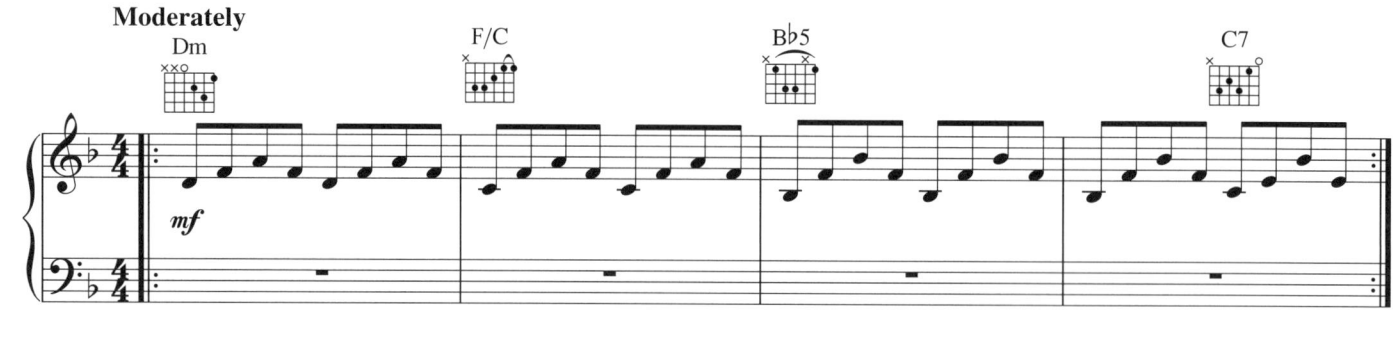
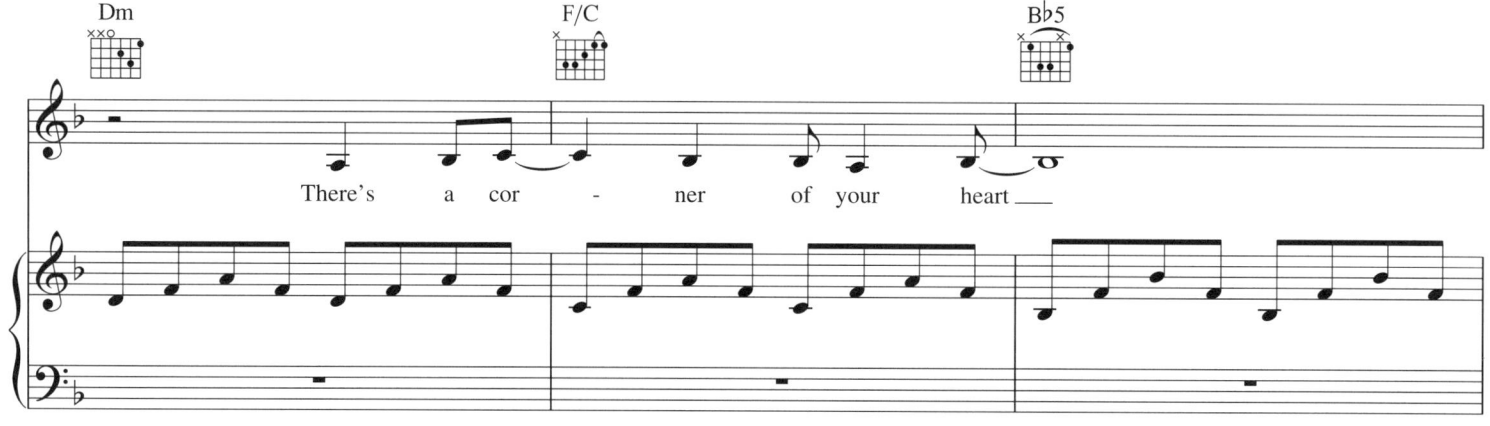

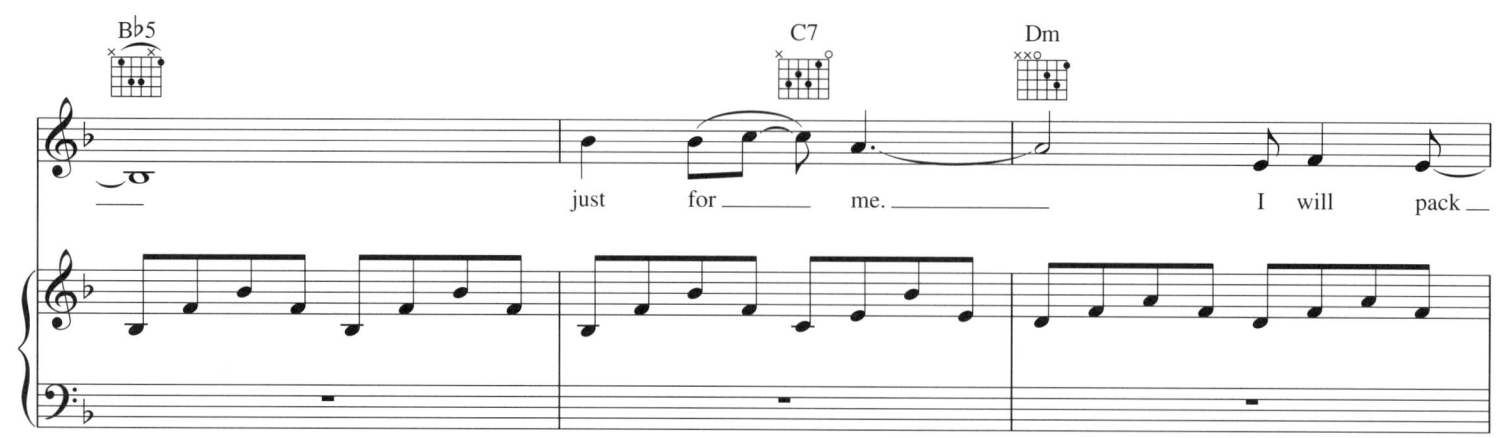

December Baby

Words and Music by
Ingrid Michaelson

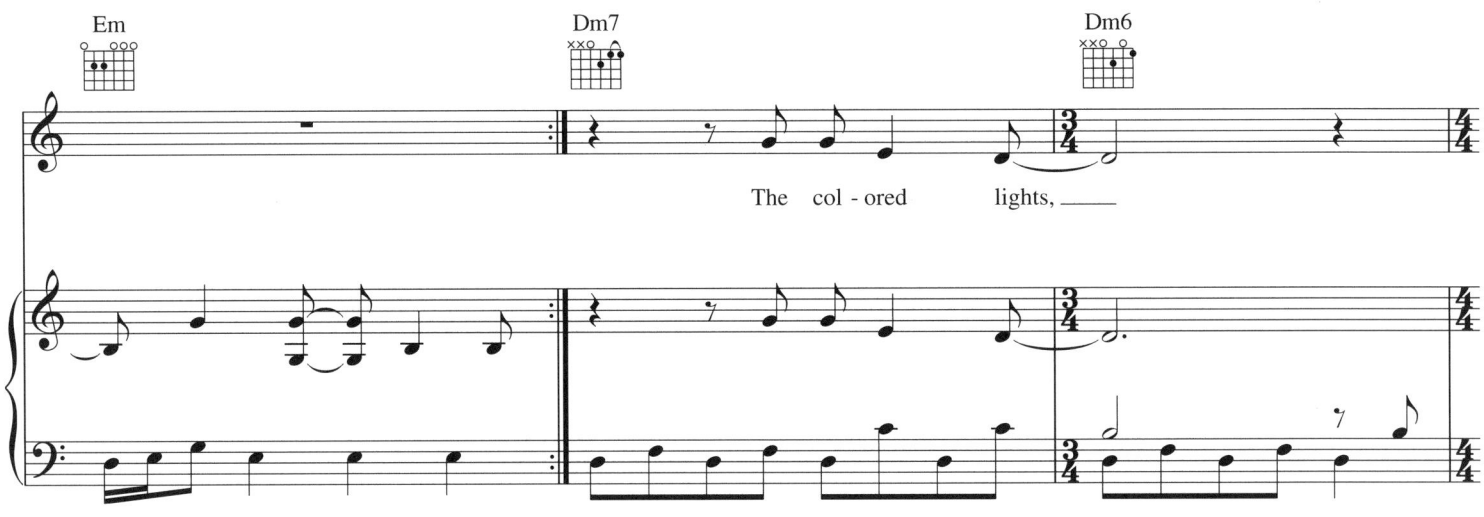
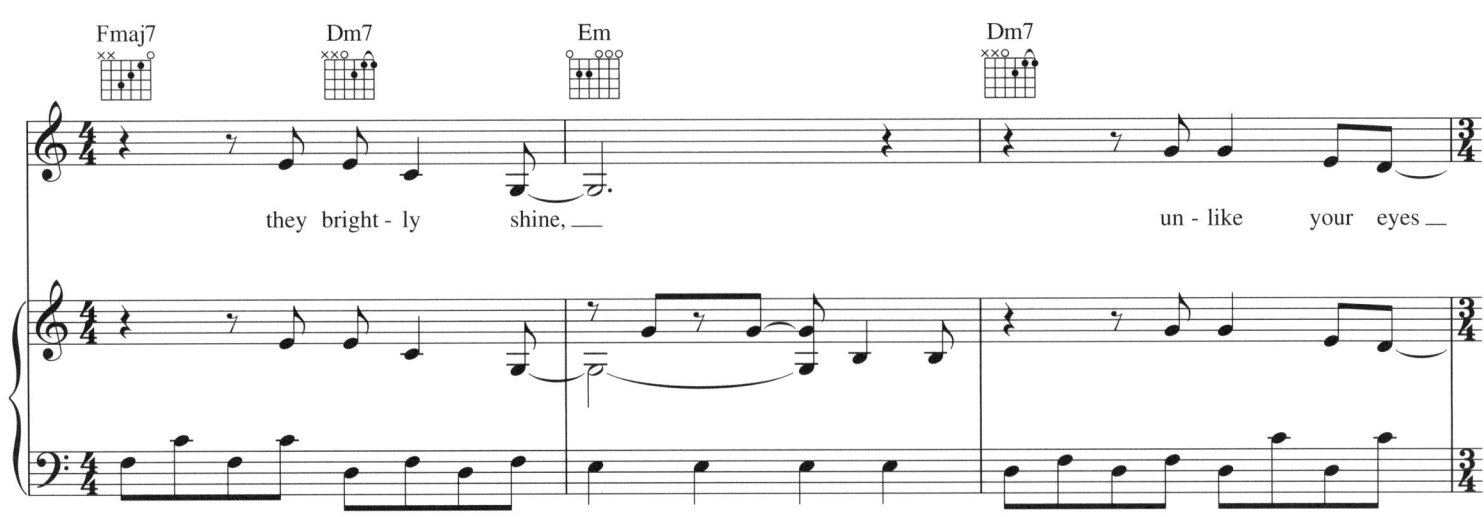

The col-ored lights, they bright-ly shine, un-like your eyes

Highway

Words and Music by
Ingrid Michaelson

Far Away

Words and Music by
Ingrid Michaelson

Be OK

Words and Music by
Ingrid Michaelson

Giving Up

Words and Music by
Ingrid Michaelson

Keep Breathing

Words and Music by
Ingrid Michaelson

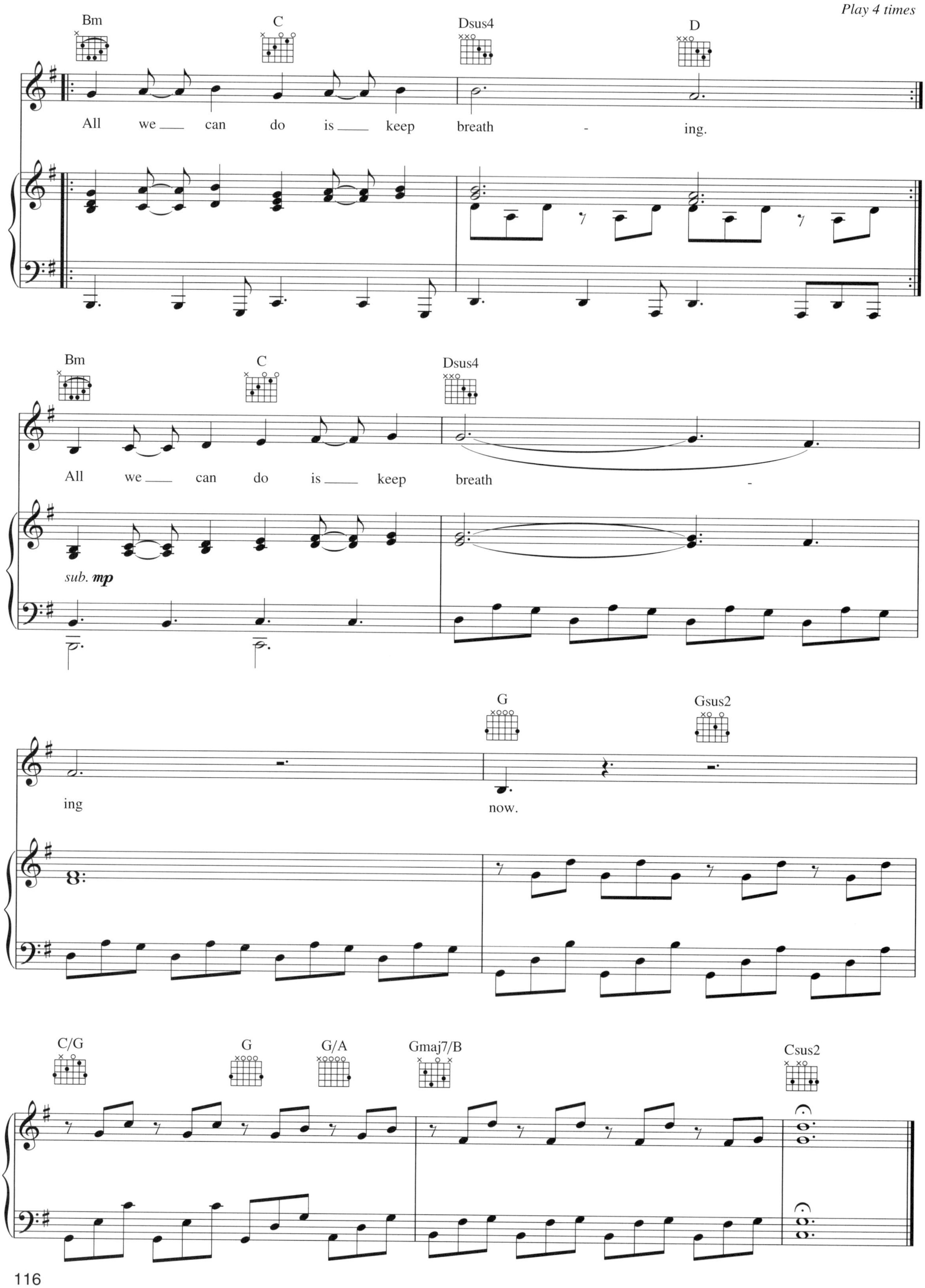
Play 4 times
Bm
C
Dsus4
D
All we can do is keep breath - ing.
Bm
C
Dsus4
All we can do is keep breath -
sub. mp
ing
G
Gsus2
now.
C/G
G
G/A
Gmaj7/B
Csus2

You and I

Words and Music by
Ingrid Michaelson

Moderately fast

Don't you wor-ry; there, my hon-ey.
you might be a bit con-fused, and

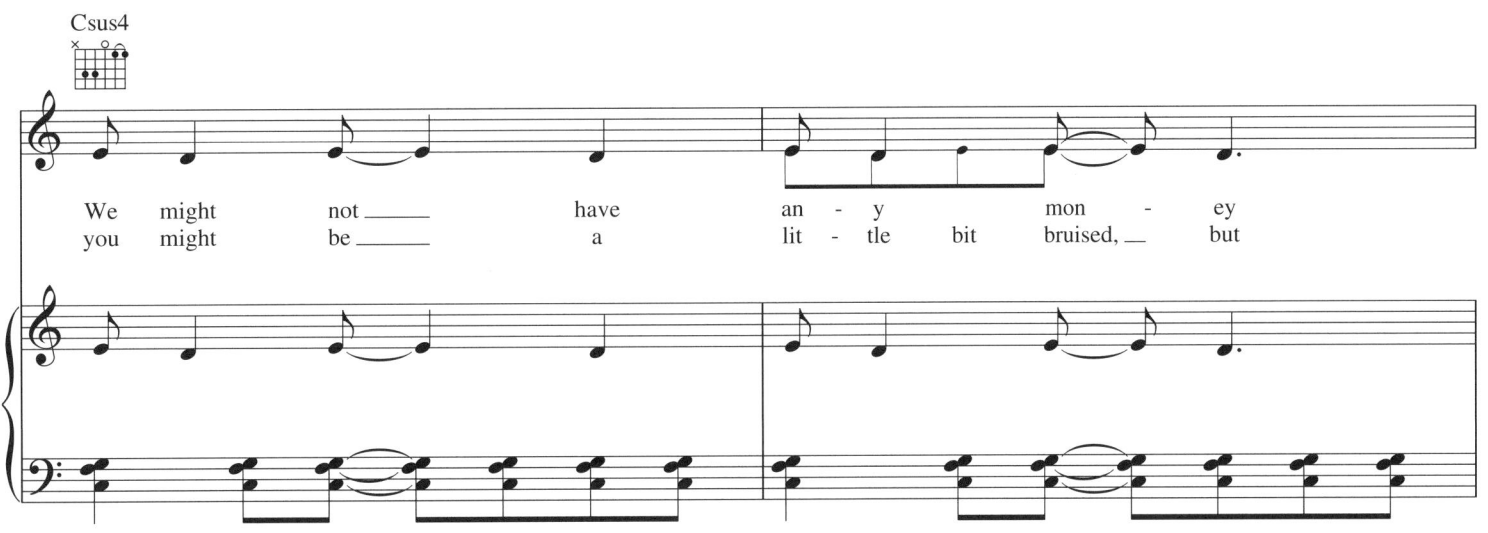

We might not have an-y mon-ey
you might be a lit-tle bit bruised, but